Reading Roundabout

Seaside
Nature

Paul Humphrey

Photography by Chris Fairclough

W
FRANKLIN WATTS
LONDON • SYDNEY

First published in 2006 by
Franklin Watts
338 Euston Road
London NW1 3BH

Franklin Watts Australia
Hachette Children's Books
Level 17/207 Kent Street
Sydney NSW 2000

WORCESTERSHIRE COUNTY COUNCIL		
553		
Bertrams		30.07.06
J577.69		£8.99

ISBN: 0 7496 6602 1 (hbk)
ISBN: 0 7496 68520 (pbk)

Dewey classification number: 577.69'9

A CIP catalogue record for this book is available
from the British Library.

Planning and production by Discovery Books Limited
Editor: Rachel Tisdale
Designer: Ian Winton
Photography: Chris Fairclough
Series advisors: Diana Bentley MA and Dee Reid MA,
Fellows of Oxford Brookes University

The author, packager and publisher would like to thank the following
people for their participation in this book: Auriel Austin-Baker; Arrandeep Bola
and family; Lucas Tisdale.

Printed in China

Contents

Seaside animals and plants

At the seaside,
there are lots of
different animals
and plants
to see.

Fish

There are tiny fish in the rock pool.

They are hard to see among the rocks.

6

7

Sea anemones

Sea anemones are found in rock pools. They look like plants but they are animals.

They catch tiny creatures with their tentacles.

Tentacles

Starfish

Starfish also live in rock pools.

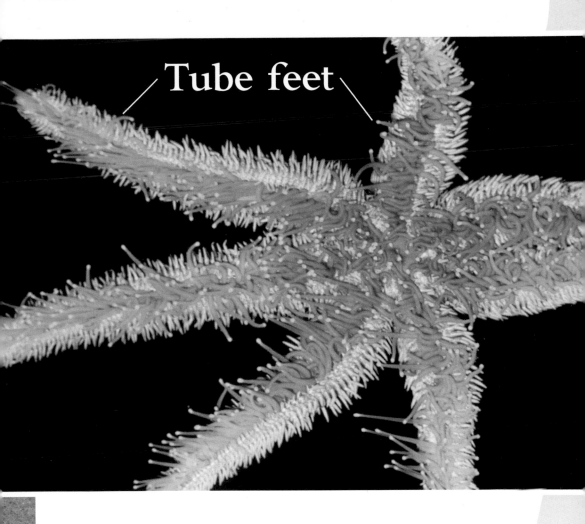

Tube feet

They move around
on tiny tube feet.

Crabs

A crab has eight legs and two sharp pincers.

Eyes

Pincer

Pincer

Legs

It runs sideways
across the beach.

Now it has climbed
on to the rocks.

Shellfish

These shellfish are called mussels. They cling to rocks.

These are winkles.
They hide inside
their curly shells.

Seaweed clings
to the rocks.

16

It has little bags of air
to help it float in
the water.

Sand dunes

The sand dunes are covered with grass. The grass stops the sand blowing away.

19

Lugworms

This looks like

a worm...

...but it is a curly
sand cast made
by this lugworm.

Seagulls

There are lots of seagulls looking for food. What do you think they will find to eat?

Word bank

Look back for these words and pictures.

Crab

Fish
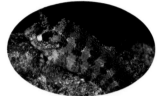

Lugworm

Mussels

Pincer

Rock pool

Sand dunes

Sea anemones

Seagull

Seaweed

Starfish

Winkle

24